AF483640

This story was written for all those who

are not perfect!

Dottie Wottie and the tinsy, winsy, little secret!

Library in Congress Cataloging-in-Publication Data.

ISBN 979-8-218-16398-3

Dottie Wottie

and the tinsy, whinsy, little secret!

written and illustrated by gina cole

"The sun is up and it is bright!"
crowed rooster with delight.

But Yooie Dooie paid no mind as he stared
at strange lumps, all of a kind.

Plumpy, earthy worms poked their heads
above the ground,
oh, what a feast they all had found!

"What's that, what's that?" said the sheep..

But confusion soon ensued
as the upturned earth seemed to move.

A clomp of dirt struck Yooie Dooie right on
the nose, and then lo and behold another,
soon he was all but covered.

"Surprise, surprise!" said the sheep.

Dottie Wottie had been digging
underground, straight across the barnyard
and around.

All were curious as could be
when Dottie Wottie popped out to see!

"Who's that, who's that?" said the sheep.

A new found friend, doesn't happen
every day, and so without delay a game of hide
and seek was underway.

Rooster counted right to ten as they all
quickly ran. One here, one there and soon the
barnyard was quite bare.

"Hide, hide!" yelled the sheep.

Yoohie Dooie hid straight behind the barn
but to no avail. Rooster, clever as could be, spotted
him and sounded the alarm.

The chickens ran to see . . .
how could this be?

"Very clever, very clever!" said the sheep.

The chickens and the sheep threw in their lot
and Rooster claimed the victory
right on the spot.!

Soon they were ready for another round
when a loud sob came from somewhere on the ground.

"What's wrong, what's wrong?" said the sheep.

Dottie's
House

Yooie Dooie quickly lent an ear as Dottie Wottie
whispered loudly so he could hear!

She tearfully confessed the tinsy, winsy, little secret
she had never shared. because her bandi
had been lost and she was scared.

"What did she say, what did she say?" said the sheep.

Dottie's House

They searched hi and lo but to no avail
it could not be found, poor Dottie underground.

Yooie Dooie gathered all, from the smallest to the
biggest, from the brightest to the thickest.
They went to Dottie Wotties house without delay
to comfort her in her dismay.

"Where is Dottie, where is Dottie?" said the sheep.

Dottie's ♥ House

Each one had flaws of one kind or another
for Dottie to discover.

Suddenly she dropped her hand from off her
nose and there it was . . . a spot, a tinsy,
winsy, little spot that no one cared about, yes,
her tinsy, winsy, little secret had come out!

"Be kind, be kind!" said the sheep.

Dottie's House

Now Dottie Wottie was finally at ease as she saw
her barnyard friends were just like her,
imperfect as could be.

A day like no other came about,
as they lived happily ever after, until now!

"Happy day, happy day!" said the sheep.

The End

Dottie's
House